P9-DNL-354

FREE PUBLIC LIBRARY
OF LIVINGSTON
LIVINGSTON, NEW JERSEY, 07039

LIFE IN THE SPIRIT

LIFE IN THE SPIRIT

Reflections, Meditations, Prayers

MOTHER TERESA OF CALCUTTA

Edited by Kathryn Spink

1817

HARPER & ROW, PUBLISHERS, San Francisco
Cambridge, Hagerstown, New York, Philadelphia
London, Mexico City, São Paulo, Sydney

Free Public Library
Livingston, N. J.

Unless indicated otherwise, Biblical quotations in this book are from the Authorized Version of the Holy Bible.

This book was first published in England with the title *In the Silence of the Heart* by SPCK, London, 1983.

LIFE IN THE SPIRIT. Selection and arrangement. Copyright © Kathryn Spink 1983. All rights reserved. Printed in the United States of America. No part of this book may be used or reproduced in any manner whatsoever without written permission except in the case of brief quotations embodied in critical articles and reviews. For information address Harper & Row, Publishers, Inc., 10 East 53rd Street, New York, NY 10022. Published simultaneously in Canada by Fitzhenry & Whiteside, Limited, Toronto.

FIRST U.S. EDITION

Library of Congress Cataloging in Publication Data

Teresa, Mother, 1910–
  LIFE IN THE SPIRIT.

  1. Meditations.   2. Prayers.   3. Teresa, Mother,
1910–   I. Spink, Kathryn.   II. Title.
BX2182.2.T394   1983   242   82-48938
ISBN 0-06-066021-X

83   84   85   86   87   10   9   8   7   6   5   4   3   2   1

EDITOR'S NOTE

I would like to express my thanks not only to Mother Teresa but also to the many Co-Workers who have helped to make this book possible. Meditations and prayers have not been individually acknowledged, but for the general guidance of the reader Mother Teresa's own words appear in bold type and those of the Co-Workers and others associated with her work in ordinary type.

My secret is quite simple. I pray and through my prayer I become one in love with Christ, and see that praying to him is to love him, and that means to fulfil his words. Remember the words of St Matthew's Gospel:

I was hungry and you gave me no food,
I was thirsty and you gave me no drink,
I was a stranger and you did not welcome me,
naked and you did not clothe me,
sick and in prison and you did not visit me.

(RSV)

My poor ones in the world's slums are like the suffering Christ. In them God's Son lives and dies, and through them God shows me his true face. Prayer for me means becoming twenty-four hours a day at one with the will of Jesus to live for him, through him and with him.

If we pray
   we will believe
If we believe
   we will love
If we love
   we will serve.

Only then can we put
   our love for God
   into living action
Through service of Christ
   in the distressing
   disguise of the Poor.

FOREWORD

This little book is centred on different aspects of the world-wide work of Mother Teresa and her thoughts on that work. It is illuminated by texts taken from the Gospels and enriched by passages and prayers written and used by those of all religious denominations who work with Mother Teresa throughout the world. Kathryn Spink has given us a small book of great worth. It will be a lovely source of inspiration for our prayers and meditation.

Mother Teresa tells us that we all need to find God and that he cannot be found in noise and restlessness – 'God is the friend of silence'. Silently the firmament proclaims the glory of God and all nature sings his praises. In the silence of our hearts he will speak to us, if we stop talking and give him a chance, if we listen, if we are quiet. The psalmist sings: 'Be still and know that I am God'. He will speak.

Mother Teresa has said, when speaking of our need to love God: 'Thou shalt love the Lord thy God with thy whole heart, with thy whole soul and with thy whole mind. This is the commandment of the great God and he cannot command the impossible. Love is a fruit in season at all times, and within reach of every hand. Anyone may gather it, and no limit is set.' These gospel-based meditations will open our hearts, speak to our souls and refresh our minds.

Everyone, Mother Teresa says, can reach this love through meditation, prayer, sacrifice and an intense inner life. Sublime advice, but how difficult to carry out! Yet Christ himself has said that when two or three are gathered together he will be there with them – not a large crowd needed, not a proper congregation, just two or three and he will be there. That is not so difficult or so intimidating. That gathering can even be together at home. The fruits of love can be gathered in by small groups of friends praying and meditating together. Fruits, however, are varied to taste – some are sweet, some bitter-sweet – and so is love. The bitter-sweetness of love is sacrifice, self-denial, forgetting self, pain. As the priest breaks the bread in the Eucharist for all to share, love necessitates breaking to share. Christ to prove his love for us died on the cross, a mother in childbirth has to suffer and so real love means suffering and sacrifice. But if we are prepared to make that sacrifice the fruits of love are ready for our gathering and no limits are set. From the prayer and meditation of the two or three with him will come forth other fruits of love: support in prayer, comfort for the troubled, growth of understanding, compassion, forgiveness, deepening of community, and faith and hope.

'Love to pray,' says Mother Teresa, 'feel often during the day the need for prayer and take trouble to pray' . . . an intense inner life is there for our gathering and no limits are set.

My prayer would be that all who read this beautiful book and meditate upon the texts will grow in ever-deepening love for God our Father and in ever more

4

understanding love for one another, our brothers and our sisters, his sons and daughters. This way is love, is peace, is joy.

ANN BLAIKIE
International Link for the
Co-Workers of Mother Teresa

*In the beginning was the Word, and the Word was
with God, and the Word was God. The same was in
the beginning with God. All things were made by him;
and without him was not anything made that was
made. In him was life; and the life was the light of
men. And the light shineth in darkness; and the
darkness comprehended it not.*

JOHN 1.1 – 5

And the Word was made flesh and dwelt among us.

JOHN 1.14

Often you see small and big wires, new and old,
cheap and expensive electric cables up – they
alone are useless and until the current passes
through them there will be no light. The wire is
you and me. The current is God. We have the
power to let the current pass through us and use
us to produce the light of the world or we can
refuse to be used and allow the darkness to spread.
My prayer is with each one of you and I pray that
each one of you will be holy, and so spread God's
love, everywhere you go. Let his light of truth be
in every person's life so that God can continue
loving the world through you and me.

Put your heart into being a bright light.

Charity for the poor we love because it is in them
that today we find Jesus, the Word incarnate, is
like a living flame; the drier the fuel, the brighter
it burns – that is our hearts must be separated

from earthly motives and united to the will of God.

The more united we are to God, the greater will be our love and readiness to serve the poor wholeheartedly. Much depends on this unison of hearts.

Today, more than ever, we need to pray for the light to perceive the word of God, for the love to accept the will of God, for the way to do the will of God.

Jesus Christ came as the light of the world and those who follow him are called upon to spread that light which is the life of men. The image of the light of truth and life radiating in a world beset by darkness is one which recurs throughout the Gospels and indeed throughout the vocabulary of so many of the world's great religions. Yet, paradoxically, it would seem that there are two darknesses or perhaps two uses for the same darkness. There is the darkness of sin and death and that darkness which enables us to become like the little children we are told we must resemble in order to enter the kingdom of heaven. It is the blind man who is prepared to place himself completely in the hands of God, to be led like a little child. Perhaps this is why, in order to raise our level of service, God plunges us into darkness. We can then learn to rely on God alone and so become the effective channels for a light which comes, not from us but from God himself.

Dear Lord, help me to spread thy fragrance everywhere I go. Flood my soul with thy spirit and life. Penetrate and possess my whole being so utterly that all my life may only be a radiance of thine. Shine through me, and be so in me that every soul I come in contact with may feel thy presence in my soul.

Let them look up and see no longer me, but only thee, O Lord! Stay with me, and then I shall begin to shine as thou shinest; so to shine as to be a light to others.

The light O Lord will be all from thee; none of it will be mine; it will be thou, shining on others through me. Let me thus praise thee in the way thou dost love best, by shining on those around me.

Let me preach thee without preaching, not by words but by my example, by the catching force, the sympathetic influence of what I do, the evident fullness of the love my heart bears to thee. Amen

Adapted by Mother Teresa from the
prayer by *Cardinal Newman*

He was in the world, and the world was made by him,
and the world knew him not. He come unto his own,
and his own received him not.

JOHN 1.10–11

Today, once more, when Jesus comes amongst his own, his own don't know him! He comes in the rotten bodies of our poor: he comes even in the rich choked by their own riches. He comes in the loneliness of their hearts, and when there is no one to love them. Jesus comes to you and me and often, very, very often, we pass him by.

After working many years among the dying, the sick, the crippled, the handicapped and mentally deficient men, women and children, I have come to one conclusion only. As I have tried to feel with the people their suffering, I have come to the understanding of what Jesus felt when he came amongst his own and they didn't want him.

Today Christ is in people who are unwanted, unemployed, uncared for, hungry, naked and homeless. They seem useless to the state or to society and nobody has time for them. It is you and I as Christians, worthy of the love of Christ if our love is true, who must find them and help them. They are there for the finding.

Everywhere we find lonely people who are at times only known by the number of their room. Where are we? Do we really know that these persons exist at all? Maybe next door to us there is a blind man who would be happy if we would be ready to read the newspaper for him; maybe there is a rich person who has no one to visit him. He has plenty of things, he is really drowned in them but there is no human touch and he needs that touch.

Some time back a very rich man came and told me: 'This I give you for somebody to come to my house. I am nearly half-blind, my wife is nearly mental, our children have all gone abroad and we are dying of loneliness.'

They are people longing for the loving sound of a human voice.

These are the people that we must know. This is Jesus yesterday and today and tomorrow that you and I must know who they are. That knowledge will lead us to love them and love to be of service to them. Let us not be satisfied with just giving money. Money is not enough. They need our hands to serve them, they need our hearts to love them. The religion of Christ is love, the spreading of love, and to be able to give love we must pray.

Don't search for God in far lands – he is not there. He is close to you. He is with you. Just keep the lamp burning and you will always see him. Watch and pray. Keep kindling the lamp and you will see his love and you will see how sweet is the Lord you love.

Lord, open our eyes,
That we may see you in our brothers and sisters.

Lord, open our ears,
That we may hear the cries of the hungry, the cold,
the frightened, the oppressed.

Lord, open our hearts,
That we may love each other as you love us.

Renew in us your spirit
Lord, free us and make us one.

Inasmuch as ye have done it unto one of the least of these my brethren, ye have done it unto me.

MATT. 25.40

For I was an hungred, and ye gave me no meat:
I was thirsty, and ye gave me no drink:
I was a stranger, and ye took me not in:
naked, and ye clothed me not:
sick, and in prison, and ye visited me not.

MATT. 25.42–3

God has identified himself with the hungry, the sick, the naked, the homeless; hunger not only for bread, but for love, for care, to be somebody to someone; nakedness, not of clothing only, but nakedness of that compassion that very few people give to the unknown; homelessness, not only just for a shelter made of stone but that homelessness that comes from having no one to call your own.

Let each of us, as we have resolved to become a true child of God, a carrier of God's love, let us love others as God has loved each one of us, for Jesus has said love one another as I have loved you.

The spiritual poverty of the western world is much greater than the physical poverty of our people. You in the West have millions of people who suffer such terrible loneliness and emptiness. They feel unloved and unwanted.

These people are not hungry in the physical sense but they are in another way. They know they need something more than money, yet they don't know what it is. What they are missing really is a living relationship with God.

Today, the poor are hungry for bread and rice – and for love and the living word of God.

The poor are thirsty – for water and for peace, truth and justice.

The poor are homeless – for a shelter made of bricks, and for a joyful heart that understands, covers, loves.

The poor are naked – for clothes, for human dignity and compassion for the naked sinner.

They are sick – for medical care, and for that gentle touch and a warm smile.

The 'shut-in', the unwanted, the unloved, the alcoholics, the dying destitutes, the abandoned and the lonely, the outcasts and the untouchables, the leprosy sufferers – all those who are a burden to human society – who have lost all hope and faith in life – who have forgotten how to smile – who have lost the sensibility of the warm hand-touch of love and friendship – they look to us for comfort. If we turn our back on them, we turn it on Christ, and at the hour of our death we shall be judged if we have recognized Christ in them, and on what we have done for and to them. There will only be two ways, 'come' or 'go'.

Therefore, I appeal to every one of you – poor

and rich, young and old – to give your own hands to serve Christ in his poor and your hearts to love him in them. They may be far or near, materially poor or spiritually poor, hungry for love and friendship, ignorant of the riches of the love of God for them, homeless for want of a home made of love in your heart; and since love begins at home maybe Christ is hungry, naked, sick or homeless in your own heart, in your family, in your neighbours, in the country you live in, in the world.

WHO ARE THE POOR?

The poor are the materially and the spiritually destitute
The poor are the hungry and the thirsty
The poor are those who need clothing
The poor are the homeless and the harbourless
The poor are the sick
The poor are the physically and mentally handicapped
The poor are the aged
The poor are those imprisoned
The poor are the lonely
The poor are the ignorant and the doubtful
The poor are the sorrowful
The poor are the comfortless
The poor are the helpless
The poor are the persecuted
The poor are those who suffer injustice
The poor are the ill-mannered
The poor are the bad-tempered

The poor are the sinners and the scoffers
The poor are those who do us wrong
The poor are the unwanted, the outcasts of society
The poor are somehow or other – we ourselves

Christ came into the world to put charity in its proper perspective.

The vision which Mother Teresa holds out to us is that, in the broken bodies and broken spirits of the outcasts, the destitute and the poor we encounter our Lord, just as surely as we encounter him in the broken bread of the Eucharist. Seen from this standpoint every broken person becomes of infinite value. They are not just objects of pity – something less than we are to be helped. Each one is a 'marvellous' person because our Lord's love is such that he has identified himself for all time with the broken and outcast. He is closer to them than they are to themselves, and in recognizing him in them we enable them to recognize their truest and deepest selves.

Lord, shake away my indifference and insensitivity to the plight of the poor. When I meet you hungry, thirsty or as a stranger, show me how I can give you food or quench your thirst or receive you in my home – and in my heart. Show me how I can serve you in the least of your brothers.

I and my Father are one.

It is not possible to engage in the direct apostolate without being a soul at prayer. We must be aware of oneness with Christ, as he was aware of oneness with his Father. Our activity is truly apostolic only in so far as we permit him to work in us and through us, with his power, with his desire, with his love. We must be holy, not because we want to feel holy, but because Christ must be able to live his life fully in us. We are to be all love, all faith, all purity, for the sake of the poor we serve, and once we have learned to seek God and his will, our contact with the poor will become the means of great sanctity to ourselves and to others.

Love to pray – feel the need to pray often during the day and take the trouble to pray. If you want to pray better, you must pray more. Prayer enlarges the heart until it is capable of containing God's gift of himself. Ask and seek and your heart will grow big enough to receive him and keep him as your own.

Pray – pray for grace, pray that you may understand how Jesus has loved you so that you may love others, and pray for us that we may not spoil God's work.

Prayer to be fruitful must come from the heart and must be able to touch the heart of God. See how Jesus taught his disciples to pray. Call God your Father, praise and glorify his name. Do his

17

will, ask for daily bread, spiritual and temporal, ask for forgiveness of your own sins and that we may forgive others – and also for the grace to be delivered from evil which is in us and around us.

Our Father who art in heaven, Hallowed be thy name.

Thy kingdom come. Thy will be done in earth, as it is in heaven.

Give us this day our daily bread.

And forgive us our trespasses, as we forgive those who trespass against us.

And lead us not into temptation, but deliver us from evil: For thine is the kingdom, the power, and the glory, for ever.   Amen

Perfect prayer does not consist in many words, but in the fervour of the desire which raised the heart of Jesus.

Be still, and know that I am God.

PSALMS 46.10

If we really want to pray we must first learn to listen, for in the silence of the heart God speaks. And to be able to see that silence, to be able to hear God, we need a clean heart, for a clean heart can see God, can hear God, can listen to God.

When it is difficult to pray we must help ourselves to do so. The first means to use is silence, for souls of prayer are souls of great silence. We cannot put ourselves directly in the presence of God if we do not practise internal and external silence.

God is the friend of silence.

Let us adore Jesus in our hearts, who spent thirty years out of thirty-three in silence, who began his public life by spending forty days in silence, who often retired alone to spend the night on a mountain in silence. He who spoke with authority, now spends his earthly life in silence. Let us adore Jesus in the eucharistic silence.

We need to find God and he cannot be found in noise and restlessness. See how nature, the trees, the flowers, the grass grow in perfect silence – see the stars, the moon and the sun, how they move in silence. Is not our mission to give God to the poor in the slums? Not a dead God but a living, loving God. The more we receive in silent prayer, the more we can give in our active life.

Silence gives us a new outlook on everything.

We need silence to be able to touch souls. The essential thing is not what we say but what God says to us and through us. Jesus is always waiting for us in silence. In that silence he will listen to us, there he will speak to our soul, and there we will hear his voice. Interior silence is very difficult but we must make the effort. In silence we will find new energy and true unity. The energy of God will be ours to do all things well. The unity of our thoughts with his thoughts, the unity of our prayers with his prayers, the unity of our actions with his actions, of our life with his life. All our words will be useless, unless they come from within – words which do not give the light of Christ increase the darkness.

Deep prayer and contemplation is a response to the love of God. It does not start with active efforts or anxious striving on our part but with love powerfully experienced. St John is quite clear on this point: 'In this is love, not that we loved God but that he loved us.' In the silence of our hearts this love is like a call which is invariably creative – evoking a response, an interior movement of the soul towards God, energy. This is the energy which enables Mother Teresa and others like her to fuse a life of prayer with a life of action. The one is totally dependent on the other. Her tremendous achievements depend for their efficacy on a receptive, listening silence.

Lord,
Teach us that even as the wonder of the stars in heaven only reveals itself in the silence of the night, so the wonder of God reveals itself in the silence of the soul. That in the silence of our hearts we may see the scattered leaves of all the universe bound by love.

Adapted from the Bhagavad Gita

How much we can learn from our Lady. She was so humble because she was all for God. She was full of grace and she made use of the almighty power that was in her – the grace of God.

The most beautiful part of our Lady was that, when Jesus came into her life, immediately she went in haste to Elizabeth to give Jesus to her and her son. And we read in the Gospel that the child 'leapt with joy' at this first contact with Christ. Our Lady was the most wonderful wire. She allowed God to fill her to the brim, so by her surrender, 'be it unto me according to thy word', she became full of grace which she went to pass on to John. So let us ask God to use us now to go round the world, especially in our own communities and continue connecting the wires of the hearts of men to the current, Jesus.

Mary can teach us silence – how to keep all things in our hearts as she did, to pray in the silence of our hearts.

Mary can teach us kindness – she went in haste to serve Elizabeth. They have no wine she told Jesus at Cana. Let us, like her, be aware of the needs of the poor, be they spiritual or material and let us, like her, give generously of the love and grace we are granted.

Mary will teach us humility – though full of grace yet only the handmaid of the Lord, she

22

stands as one of us at the foot of the cross, a sinner needing redemption. Let us, like her, touch the dying, the poor, the lonely and the unwanted according to the graces we have received and let us not be ashamed or slow to do the humble work.

Lord, in her humility Mary acknowledged your all-powerful wisdom. Though troubled by the angel's message and unaware of its full meaning, she accepted it as the 'servant of the Lord'.

But what of me, Lord?

Do I listen to what you have to tell me or am I too busy talking?

Do I seek to know your plan for me or am I too concerned with shaping my own destiny?

And when I receive the answer to my prayers do I run from it or do I commend myself into your hands and give generously of the gifts you have granted me?

Lord, into your hands I commend my spirit.

Be ye therefore perfect, even as your Father which is in heaven is perfect.

MATT. 5.48

Holiness is not the luxury of the few but a simple duty for you and me so let us be holy as our Father in heaven is holy. St Thomas says: 'Sanctity consists in nothing else but a firm resolve' – the heroic act of a soul abandoning itself to God.

Our progress in holiness depends on God and on ourselves – on God's grace and on our will to be holy. We must have a real living determination to reach holiness. 'I will be a saint' means I will despoil myself of all that is not God, I will strip my heart of all created things, I will live in poverty and detachment, I will renounce my will, my inclinations, my whims and fancies, and make myself a willing slave to the will of God . . .

Give yourself fully to God. He will use you to accomplish great things on the condition that you believe much more in his love than in your own weakness.

St Augustine says: 'Fill yourselves first and then only will you be able to give to others.' If we really want God to fill us, we must empty ourselves through humility of all that is selfishness in us.

We must not attempt to control God's actions. We must not count the stages in the journey he would have us make. We must not desire a clear perception of our advance along the road, nor know precisely where we are on the way of holiness. I ask him to make a saint of me, yet I must leave to him the choice of that saintliness itself and still more the choice of the means which lead to it.

Make sure that you let God's grace work in your souls by accepting whatever he gives you, and giving him whatever he takes from you. True holiness consists in doing God's will with a smile.

Lord, make me a saint according to your own heart, meek and humble.

> *What things soever ye desire, when ye pray, believe that ye receive them, and ye shall have them.*
>
> MARK 11.24

If we really fully belong to God, then we must be at his disposal and we must trust in him. We must never be preoccupied with the future. There is no reason to be so. God is there.

There has not been one single day that we have refused somebody, that we did not have food, that we did not have a bed or something, and we deal with thousands of people. We have 53,000 lepers and yet never one has been sent away because we did not have. It is always there, though we have no salaries, no income, no nothing, we receive freely and give freely. This has been such a beautiful gift of God. In Calcutta alone we cope for 7,000 people every day and if one day we do not cook they do not eat. And this, one Friday morning Sister came and told me: 'Mother, Friday – Saturday, there is no food, we will have to tell the people we have nothing to give today and tomorrow.'

I had no words, I had nothing to say to her, but by nine o'clock the Government for some unknown reason closed all the schools, and all the bread that would have been given to the children was sent to us and our children and our 7,000 people ate bread and bread for two days. They had never eaten so much bread in their lives. Nobody in the whole city knew why the schools were closed, but I knew. I knew the delicate thoughtfulness of God – such a delicate love.

Our dependence on Divine Providence is a firm and lively faith that God can and will help us. That he can is evident, because he is almighty; that he will is certain because he promised it in so many passages of Holy Scripture and because he is infinitely faithful to all his promises. Christ encourages us to have this confidence in these words: 'Whatever you ask in prayer, believe that you have received it, and it will be yours' (RSV). The apostle St Peter also commands us to throw all cares upon the Lord who provides for us. And why should God not care for us since he sent us his Son and with him all? St Augustine says: 'How can you doubt that God will give you good things since he vouchsafed to assume evil for you?'

This must give us confidence in the Providence of God who preserves even the birds and the flowers. Surely if God feeds the young ravens which cry to him, if he nourishes the birds which neither sow nor reap nor gather into barns; if he vests the flowers of the field so beautifully, how much more will he care for men whom he has made in his own image and likeness and adopted as his children, if we only act as such, keep his commandments and have confidence in him.

I don't want the work to become a business but to remain a work of love. I want you to have that complete confidence that God won't let us down. Take him at his word and seek first the kingdom of heaven, and all else will be added on.

It is impossible to confront the problem of hunger in a city like Calcutta with only a handful of young men and girls of good will, without money and without know-how. But given that it is God who calls them (the Missionaries of Charity), they tackle it with joy and faith. They start by doing whatever they can and God takes care of the rest. It does not matter if the man whom they are nursing resells the medicine that he gets from them. They give it to him with a prayer and so God will be with this man much more than they can ever be. It does not greatly matter if they do not have the necessary vaccine for the treatment of this sick woman, because they give her what has been given to them free of charge – the love of God and the few medicines they possess. God will take care of this sick woman. To human eyes this trust in God seems carried to excess, but it is the touchstone of the whole work of Mother Teresa. Her favourite saying is, 'If God wants something, it will be done'. This is how she can afford to make use of only 'small means'. She dares remain 'small' even when faced with the enormity of the work. This weakness is her strength since it is the source of peace and serenity, where others might give up through discouragement and bitterness.

Paul Chetcuti SJ
(from *Choosing to Serve the Destitute*)

> Take, Oh Lord and receive
> All my liberty, my memory
> my understanding and my will,
> all that I have and possess.
> You have given them to me

To you, Oh Lord, I restore them.
All things are yours
Dispose of them according to your will.
Give me your love and your grace
For this is enough for me.

Nevertheless I live; yet not I, but Christ liveth in me.

GAL. 2.20

The life of the soul is the life of Jesus Christ himself. Jesus with the Father and the Holy Spirit is the efficient cause of sanctifying grace in our souls. By this life, Jesus Christ imparts to me his Spirit. He becomes the principle of a higher activity which prompts me, if I do not put any obstacle in the way to think, judge, love, suffer and work with him, by him and like him. So our exterior actions become the manifestations of that life of Jesus in me, and I realize the ideal of St Paul: 'Nevertheless I live; yet not I, but Christ liveth in me.' If we learn this interior life, the words of our Lord will be fulfilled in our regard: 'He that abideth in me, and I in him, the same bringeth forth much fruit.'

'I kept the Lord ever before my eyes because he is ever at my right hand that I may not slip', says the psalmist. God is within me with a more intimate presence than that whereby I am in myself: in him we live and move and have our being. It is he who gives life to all, that gives power and being to all that exists. But for his sustaining presence, all things would cease to be and fall back into nothingness. Consider that you are in God, surrounded and encompassed by God, swimming in God.

The true interior life makes the active life burn forth and consume everything. It makes us find

Jesus in the dark holes of the slums in the most pitiful miseries of the poor – the God-man naked on the cross.

Our lives to be fruitful must be full of Christ. To be able to bring his peace, joy and love we must have it ourselves for we cannot give what we have not got, like the blind leading the blind. The poor in the slums are without Jesus and we have the privilege of entering their homes. What they think of us does not matter but what we are to them does matter. To go to the poor and the sick merely for the sake of going will not be enough to draw them to Jesus. If we are preoccupied with ourselves and our own affairs, we will not be able to live up to this ideal.

We are but instruments that God deigns to use. These instruments bring forth fruit in the measure that they are united to God, for St Paul says: 'I have planted, Apollos watered; but God gave the increase.' We obtain grace in proportion to our sanctity, to our fervour and to our degree of union with our Lord.

The richest and most fortunate creature in the whole of creation is undoubtedly man. In the very beginning you, Lord, created man in your own image to have dominion over all other creatures.

Each man is unique. I am unique, Lord – You have made me unrepeatable. There has never been and never will be another me among all the millions of people who belong to the human race. You have made me unique and you have bestowed on me talents and graces. There is in me all the potential to become like your Son, Jesus Christ – the perfect man. You have given me the potential to develop the life of Christ in me. Help me to be aware of this potential and to develop it through contact with others.

Lord by thy Grace

Let the poor seeing me be drawn to Christ and invite him to enter their homes and their lives.

Let the sick and the suffering find in me a real angel of comfort and consolation.

Let the little ones of the streets cling to me because I remind them of him, the friend of all little ones.

*Though I speak with the tongues of men and of angels,
and have not charity, I am become as sounding brass, or
a tinkling cymbal. And though I have the gift of
prophecy, and understand all mysteries, and all
knowledge; and though I have all faith, so that I could
remove mountains, and have not charity, I am nothing.*

I COR. 13.1–2

Thoughtfulness is the beginning of great sanctity.
If you learn this art of being thoughtful, you will
become more and more Christlike, for his heart
was meek and he always thought of the needs of
others – our lives to be beautiful must be full of
thought for others. Jesus went about doing good.
Our Lady did nothing else in Cana but thought of
the needs of the others and made their needs
known to Jesus. The thoughtfulness of Jesus and
Mary and Joseph was so great that it made Nazareth the abode of God most high. If we also have
that kind of thoughtfulness for each other, our
homes would really become the abode of God
most high.

The quickest and the surest way is the 'tongue'
– use it for the good of others. If you think well of
others, you will also speak well of others and to
others. From the abundance of the heart the mouth
speaketh. If your heart is full of love, you will
speak of love.

Violence of the tongue is very real – sharper
than any knife, wounding and creating bitterness
that only the grace of God can heal.

Lord, teach me to speak not as a sounding brass or a tinkling cymbal, but with love,

Grant me understanding and the faith that moves mountains, but with love,

Show me that love which is ever patient and ever kind; never jealous, conceited, selfish or resentful,

The love that delights in truth, ever ready to excuse, to trust, to hope and to endure

That at the last, when all imperfect things will fade away and I shall know as I am known,

I may have been the dim, but abiding reflection of your perfect love.

Thou shalt love the Lord thy God with all thy heart,
with all thy soul, and with all thy mind.

DEUT. 6.5

This is the commandment of our great God, and he cannot command the impossible. Love is a fruit in season at all times and within the reach of every hand. Anyone may gather it and no limit is set. Everyone can reach this love through meditation, the spirit of prayer and sacrifice, by an intense inner life. Do we really live this life?

We must all fill our hearts with great love. Don't imagine that love, to be true and burning, must be extraordinary. No – what we need in our love is the continuity to love the one who loved the world so much he gave his Son. God is still love, he is still loving the world. Today God loves the world so much that he gives you and he gives me to love the world, to be his love and compassion. The world is hungry for God and when Jesus came into the world he wanted to satisfy that hunger. He made himself the Bread of Life, so small, so fragile, so helpless, and as if that was not enough, he made himself the hungry one, the naked one, the homeless one, so that we can satisfy his hunger for love – for our human love, not something extraordinary but our human love.

Pray lovingly like children, with an earnest desire to love much and make loved the love that is not loved.

Let us thank God for all his love for us, in so many ways and in so many places.

Let us in return, as an act of gratitude and adoration, determine to love him.

St Teresa of Avila teaches that prayer does not consist in thinking much but in loving much. To pray is to love God and to love is to give. Whatever we possess is not ours: we are only the stewards of all that we possess and the only adequate gift we can offer is ourselves. There is no substitute for it. Nothing less will do.

Give me, O God, the most blessed gift I know, a heart full of Christ's love.

He that saith he is in the light, and hateth his brother
is in darkness even until now.
He that loveth his brother abideth in the light, and
there is none occasion of stumbling in him.

1 JOHN 2.9–10

'Love one another, even as I have loved you.' These words should be not only a light to us, but also a flame consuming the selfishness which prevents the growth of holiness. Jesus loved us to the end, to the very limit of love, the cross. Love must come from within – from our union with Christ – an outpouring of our love for God. Loving should be as normal to us as living and breathing, day after day until our death. The Little Flower said: 'When I act and think with charity, I feel it is Jesus who works within me. The closer I am united with him, the more I love all the other dwellers in Carmel.' To understand this and practise it we need much prayer, which unites us with others. Our works of charity are nothing but the overflow of our love for God from within.

St John says something very strange: how can you love God whom you don't see if you don't love your neighbour – one another – whom you see? And he uses very strange words: 'If you say you love God and don't love your neighbour, you are a liar.'

Because we cannot see Christ we cannot express our love to him, but our neighbours we can always see, and we can do to them what, if we saw him, we would like to do to Christ.

God gives us that great strength and the great joy of loving those he has chosen. Do we use it? Where do we use it first? Jesus said love one another. He didn't say love the world, he said love one another – right here, my brother, my neighbour, my husband, my wife, my child, the old ones. Our Sisters are working around the world and I have seen all the trouble, all the misery, all the suffering. From where did it come? It has come from lack of love and lack of prayer. There is no coming together in the family, praying together, coming together, staying together. Love begins at home and we will find the poor even in our own home. We have a house in London. Our Sisters there work at night and one night they went out to pick up the people on the streets. They saw a young man there late at night, lying in the street, and they said, 'You should not be here, you should be with your parents', and he said, 'When I go home my mother does not want me because I have long hair. Every time I go home she pushes me out.' By the time they came back he had taken an overdose and they had to take him to hospital. I could not help thinking it was quite possible his mother was busy, with the hunger of our people of India, and there was her own child hungry for her, hungry for her love, hungry for her care and she refused it.

It is easy to love the people far away. It is not

always easy to love those close to us. It is easier to give a cup of rice to relieve hunger than to relieve the loneliness and pain of someone unloved in our own home. Bring love into your home for this is where our love for each other must start.

Lord, keep us faithful to each other – in your love. Let nothing, let nobody separate us from your love and the love we must bear for each other.   Amen

*Yea, a man may say, Thou hast faith, and I have
works: show me thy faith without thy works, and I
will show thee my faith by my works.*

Jas. 2.18

What will it profit, if a man says he has faith, but
does not have works? Can the faith alone save
him? If a brother or sister is naked and in want of
daily food, and one of you says to them, 'Go in
peace, be warmed and filled', yet you do not give
them what is necessary for the body, what does it
profit? So faith too, unless it has works, is dead in
itself. But someone will say: 'You have faith and
I have works. Show me your faith without works
and I from my works will show you my faith.'

True love for our neighbour is to wish him well
and do good to him. 'My little children', St John
says, 'Let us love not in word but in deed.'

Love does not live on words, nor can it be
explained by words – especially that love which
serves him, which comes from him and which
finds him and touches him. We must reach the
heart and to reach the heart as we must do – love
is proved in deeds.

In one of the places in Melbourne I visited an old
man and nobody ever knew that he existed. I saw
his room in a terrible state, and I wanted to clean
his house and he kept on saying: 'I'm all right!' But
I repeated the same words: 'You will be more all
right if you will allow me to clean your place,' and
in the end he allowed me. There in that room there

was a beautiful lamp covered with the dirt of many years, and I asked him, 'Why do you not light your lamp?' Then I asked him, 'Will you light the lamp if the Sisters come to see you?' And the other day he sent me word: 'Tell my friend the light she has lit in my life is still burning.'

Simple acts of love and care keep the light of Christ burning.

Charles de Foucauld wrote: 'All our life, however silent it is . . . must be a witness of the Good News through example; our whole existence, whatever we are must shout the Good News from the roof-tops; our whole being must radiate Jesus . . . a life that calls Jesus, that shows Jesus, that shines like a reflection of Jesus.' And so let us proclaim that the light of love is more powerful than power, money, corruption, lies, prejudice, hypocrisy, physical or moral violence and the darkness of this world – simply by our example.

Do you want my hands, Lord, to spend the day
helping the sick and the poor who need them?
Lord, today I give you my hands.
Do you want my feet, Lord, to spend the day
visiting those who need a friend?
Lord, today I give you my feet.
Do you want my voice, Lord, to spend the day
speaking to all who need your words of love?
Lord, today I give you my voice.
Do you want my heart, Lord, to spend the day
loving everyone without exception?
Lord, today I give you my heart.

The earth is full of the goodness of the Lord.

Ps. 33.5

In the Gospel we often see one word: 'come to me all', 'he that cometh to me I will not cast out', 'suffer little children to come to me'. We must be always ready to receive, to forgive, to love and to make sure we understand what God means when he says, 'I say to you, as long as you did it to one of these my least brethren, you did it to me'. One thing will always secure heaven for us – the acts of charity and kindness with which we have filled our lives. We will never know just how much good a simple smile can do. We tell people how kind, forgiving and understanding God is but are we the living proof? Can they really see this kindness, this forgiveness, this understanding alive in us?

Be kind and merciful. Let no one ever come to you without leaving better and happier. Be the living expression of God's kindness – kindness in your face, kindness in your eyes, kindness in your smile, kindness in your warm greeting. In the slums we are the light of God's kindness to the poor. To children, to the poor, to all who suffer and are lonely, give always a happy smile. Give them not only your care but also your heart. Because of God's goodness and love every moment of our life can be the beginning of great things. Be open, ready to receive and you will find him everywhere. Every work of love brings a person face to face with God.

An old man in Calcutta once said:

'Who is this Christ of Mother Teresa's?'

'He's our Guru, old man, our Lord and our God.'

'What God is this?'

'He's a God of love, old man. He loves all of us – me and you too!'

'How could he love me, Mem Sahib? He doesn't even know me.'

'Oh yes he does! Didn't he reach right out across the city for you? Didn't he send his Sisters to the slums of Motijhil to bring you here? Doesn't he love you then, old man?'

After a pause the old man said:

'Could I love him, do you think?'

'Of course you could – it's easy to love him – we'll love him together, old man, but sleep now. We'll talk again in the morning. Sleep now, old man.'

And so a new hope was born at the very door of death.

It is a question of placing oneself in an unconditional attitude of expectation of the God who gives himself to every man in the course of his lifetime. Thus the Missionaries of Charity concentrate completely on receiving their guest generously and without conditions. This open-hearted attitude also involves the acceptance of the fellow man just as he is. It is this which is so striking in Mother Teresa's houses – everyone is welcome. Nothing is asked of the guest or patient, not even the certainty that this or that one will profit by the offered help. It is striking with what kindness the Missionaries of Charity receive the same patient several times. Once cured, the patient returns to the street and after a short time he stands at the door again, sometimes in a worse state than before. The Sisters are always ready to admit him and begin the nursing once more. It is one of the characteristics of the poorest that they cannot free themselves from this cycle. For our western mentality it contradicts all ideas of a profitable system to look after incurable people. For the Missionaries of Charity there is no incurable person. Every situation, even the most hopeless one, contains the germ of a secret promise.

Lord, give me an open heart to find you everywhere, to glimpse the heaven enfolded in a bud, and experience eternity in the smallest act of love.

We can do no great things – only small things with great love. The Sisters are doing small things: helping the children, visiting the lonely, the sick, the unwanted. In one of the houses the Sisters visit a woman living alone who was dead many days before she was found – and she was found because her body had begun to decompose. The people around her did not even know her name.

When someone told me that the Sisters had not started any big work, that they were quietly doing small things, I said that even if they helped one person, that was enough. Jesus would have died for one person, for one sinner.

You can do what I can't do. I can do what you can't do. Together we can do something beautiful for God.

Let no one glory in their success but refer all to God in deepest thankfulness; on the other hand no failure should dishearten them as long as they have done their best. God sees only our love. God will not ask how many books we have read, how many miracles we have worked, but whether we have done our best for the love of him. Have we played well? slept well? eaten well? Nothing is small for God because he is almighty, and there-

**fore each one of our actions done with and for
and through Jesus Christ is a great success.**

The trouble always begins when I start to think big of
myself – that I should be considered great, that I
should be more highly esteemed, that the work should
be more efficient, that I should help a greater number
of people, change the big structures of society – in a
word, be a real leader. Then Lord, I look at myself, at
the little I do and the less I seem to accomplish, and
I see who I really am.

Lord, in a way my life has been a way downhill, a
journey towards nothingness, towards the less. For I
know that in nothingness there is everything, that in
poverty there is wealth, that in smallness lies true
greatness. In a way there is a leadership I renounced;
at the same time there is a leadership I continued to
exercise making me live more deeply. It is a leadership
of smallness, a leadership of sharing my very life with
the marginals of society, with those who don't fit into
the system.

At the same time, Lord, I have come to know that
in reality I am not a leader of these little ones. I am
little, like them, and in seeing me little like them, they
realize that they are equal to someone who at the same
time gives them hope that they are able to be better.
While sometimes they look at me as a leader, I know
that in reality it is they who are my true leaders. They
are my direction, my inspiration, the meaning of my
whole life. When I see myself as a little one among
little ones, I come to see my true self. I continue to
understand why you, Lord, sent me here. I come to

see what a true missionary should be. I come to see that a true missionary is one who brings about a double incarnation: being one as far as possible with the people to whom he is offering his life and at the same time being one with the least – the God-man, Jesus of Nazareth. I come to realize that I cannot be one with the people if I am not one with you, Lord, who are one with me too.

Here I am, Lord – body, heart and soul.
Grant that with your love, I may be big enough to reach the world
And small enough to be at one with you.

> *Let this mind be in you, which was also in Christ
> Jesus:*
>
> *Who, being in the form of God, thought it not robbery
> to be equal with God:*
>
> *But made himself of no reputation, and took upon him
> the form of a servant, and was made in the likeness of
> men.*
>
> Phil. 2.5–7

It is beautiful to see the humility of Christ. This humility can be seen in the crib, in the exile in Egypt, in the hidden life, in the inability to make people understand him, in the desertion of his apostles, in the hatred of the Jews and all the terrible sufferings and death of his Passion and now in his permanent state of humility in the tabernacle, where he has reduced himself to such a small particle of bread that the priest can hold him with two fingers. The more we empty ourselves, the more room we give God to fill us. Let there be no pride nor vanity in the work. The work is God's work; the poor are God's poor. Work for Jesus and Jesus will work with you, pray with Jesus and Jesus will pray through you. The more you forget yourself, the more Jesus will think of you. The more you detach yourself from self, the more attached Jesus is to you.

Do not think it is a waste of time to feed the hungry, to visit and take care of the sick and the dying, to open and receive the unwanted and the homeless, for this is our love of Christ in action.

Check Out Receipt

Livingston Public Library
973-992-4600

Monday, September 24, 2018 10:18:33
AM

Item: 31792000949276
Title: Life in the spirit : reflections,
meditations, prayers
Due: 10/22/2018

Total items: 1

You just saved $30.00 by using your
library. You have saved $40.00 this past
year and $585.00 since you began using
the library!

Thank you for visiting the
Livingston Public Library!

livingston.bccls.org
(973) 992-4600

We must not drift away from the humble works, because these are the works nobody will do. It is never too small. We are so small we look at things in a small way. But God, being Almighty, sees everything great. Therefore, even if you write a letter for a blind man or you just go and sit and listen, or you take the mail for him, or you visit somebody or bring a flower to somebody – small things – or wash clothes for somebody or clean the house. Very humble work that is where you and I must be. For there are many people who can do big things. But there are very few people who will do the small things.

There may be times when we appear to be wasting our precious life and burying our talents. Our lives are utterly wasted if we use only the light of reason. Our life has no meaning unless we look at Christ in his poverty.

Today when everything is questioned and changed let us go back to Nazareth. Jesus had come to redeem the world – to teach us that love of his Father. How strange that he should spend thirty years just doing nothing, wasting his time! Not giving a chance to his personality or to his gifts, for we know that at the age of twelve he silenced the learned priests of the temple, who knew so much and so well. But when his parents found him, he went down to Nazareth and was subject to them. For thirty years we hear no more of him – so that the people were astonished when he came in public to preach, he a carpenter's son, doing just the humble work in a carpenter's shop – for thirty years!

Knowledge of God gives love and knowledge of self gives humility. Humility is nothing but truth. What have we got that we have not received? asks St Paul. If I have received everything, what good have I of my own? If we are convinced of this we will never raise our head in pride. If you are humble nothing will touch you, neither praise nor disgrace, because you know what you are. If you are blamed you will not be discouraged. If they call you a saint you will not put yourself on a pedestal.

Self-knowledge puts us on our knees.

Make us worthy, Lord, to serve our fellow men throughout the world who live and die in poverty and hunger.

Lord, grant that I may seek rather to comfort than to be comforted; to understand than to be understood; to love than to be loved; for it is by forgetting self that one finds; it is by forgiving that one is forgiven; it is by dying that one awakens to eternal life.

> *Blessed are the poor in spirit: for theirs is the kingdom of heaven.*
>
> MATT. 5.3

Our Lord gives us a living example: 'The foxes have holes, and the birds of the air have nests; but the Son of man hath not where to lay his head.' From the very first day of his human existence he was brought up in poverty, which no human being will ever be able to experience, because 'being rich he made himself poor'.

The poorest of the poor are free, happy and without the aggression of those who aspire or can aspire to many things. The poor of the third world can teach us contentment. That is something that the West does not have much of. I'll give you an example of what happened to me recently. I went out with my Sisters in Calcutta to seek out the sick and dying. We picked up about forty people that day. One woman, covered in a dirty cloth, was very ill and I could see it. So I just held her hand and tried to comfort her. She smiled weakly at me and said, 'Thank you'. Then she died. She was more concerned to give to me than to receive from me. I put myself in her place and I thought what I would have done. I am sure I would have said: 'I am dying, I am hungry, call a doctor, call a Father, call somebody.' But what she did was so beautiful. That woman was more concerned with me than I was with her.

He was a little boy of about seven years who had been brought to our Home for the Dying in Howrah. He was dying too, but with simple care he recovered and was a very lively little boy when I met him playing around the home until we could find some better place for him. I was staying there, and for two days noticed that he always had with him a cheap rubber ball that he'd got at a Christmas party. That ball was all he had in the world apart from the clothes he wore. In the evening he came up on the terrace with the ball of course and he and I began to play with it. After a few moments it bounced over the edge and he sped downstairs to recover it. Watching from the roof, I saw an older boy, a bit slow of mind, grab it and when the little boy arrived, he threw it over the wall. The little boy scaled the wall, couldn't find it and then looked up at me who was thinking what a tragedy this loss was for him. But what he did was a gesture of 'It doesn't matter', scaled back over the wall, and went off with a carefree skip and a song. I was left on the terrace to reflect on poverty of spirit, the Beatitudes and just who is rich and who is poor?

Maybe I'm crazy, but after all these years close to desperately poor people, I strongly believe that the greatest pain is not found in Calcutta or Cambodia, or El Salvador or Siberia. In these places it is the hungry belly, the sick body, the wretchedly housed family. And while we work at these points of suffering, we make an enormous mistake if we fail to recognize the richness of spirit of the people of these places and situations. Far more frightening for me are the crippled and under-nourished minds and hearts of the well-fed and well-housed and well-educated in the affluent parts of the world.

Brother Andrew M.C. (Servant General of the Missionary Brothers of Charity.)

It is not a sin to be rich. There must be a reason why some people can afford to live well. They must have worked for it. But I tell you this provokes avarice, and there comes sin. Richness is given by God and it is our duty to divide it with those less favoured.

Some time ago, a Hindu gentleman was asked: 'What is a Christian?' And he gave a very simple and a very strange answer: 'A Christian is giving.' And right from the beginning we find that it is really just giving. God loved the world so much that he gave his Son – the first great giving. Being rich he became poor for you and me. He gave himself totally. But that was not enough. He wanted to give something more – to give us the chance to give to him. So he made himself the hungry one, the naked one so that we could give to him.

Let us not be satisfied with just giving money; money is not enough for money one can get. The poor need our hands to serve them, they need our hearts to love them. Let us give, not from our abundance but until it hurts. Let us make ourselves poor for him.

Lord, when I think that my heart is overflowing with

love and realize in a moment's honesty that it is only myself that I love in the loved one,
Deliver me from myself.

Lord, when I think that I have given all that I have to give and realize in a moment's honesty that it is I who am the recipient,
Deliver me from myself.

Lord, when I have convinced myself that I am poor and realize in a moment's honesty that I am rich in pride and envy,
Deliver me from myself.

And, Lord, when the Kingdom of Heaven merges deceptively with the kingdoms of this world,
Let nothing satisfy me but God.

Then saith he to Thomas, Reach hither thy finger, and behold my hands; and reach hither thy hand, and thrust it into my side: and be not faithless, but believing.

JOHN 20.27

I don't want you to give from your abundance. I want you to touch to understand. We are not social workers but contemplatives in the world. In our work amongst the poorest of the poor we are touching Jesus all the twenty-four hours.

The very poor do not need words but actions and I cannot analyse systems, economic patterns and ideologies. I recognize that each person has a conscience and must respond to its calling. Mine is this. So many times I have been told that I must not offer fishes to men but rods so that they can fish for themselves. Ah! my God! So often they do not have the strength to hold the rods. Giving them fish I help them to recover the strength necessary for the fishing of tomorrow. There are in the world those who struggle for justice and for human rights and who try to change structures. We are not inattentive to this but our daily contact is with men who do not even have a piece of bread to eat. Our mission is to look at the problem more individually and not collectively. We care for a person and not a multitude. We seek the person with whom Jesus Christ identified himself when he said, 'I was hungry, I was sick'.

To know the problem of poverty intellectually is not to understand it. It is not by reading, taking a walk in the slums, admiring and regretting that we come to understand it and to discover what it has of bad and good. We have to dive into it, live it, share it.

A girl came from outside India to join the Missionaries of Charity. We have a rule that new arrivals must go to the Home for the Dying. So I told this girl: 'You saw Father during Holy Mass, with what love and care he touched Jesus in the Host. Do the same when you go to the Home for the Dying, because it is the same Jesus you will find there in the broken bodies of our poor.' And they went. After three hours the newcomer came back and said to me with a big smile – I have never seen a smile quite like that: 'Mother, I have been touching the body of Christ for three hours.' And I said to her: 'How?' She replied: 'When we arrived there, they brought a man who had fallen into a drain and been there for some time. He was covered with wounds and dirt and maggots, and I cleaned him and I knew I was touching the body of Christ.' That was very beautiful.

It is not always easy to believe that Christ is present in our fellow man – in the disagreeable individual who is physically repulsive, apparently spiritually barren and mentally far removed from our own 'wavelength'. Intellectually the whole business is incomprehensible and at the very least, highly improbable, and if we stop to rationalize the result is inevitably doubt. In the face of such doubts, there is a certain comfort to be derived from the fact that the risen Christ met with the same reservations some two thousand years ago. The response to such disbelief was the invitation to touch and that invitation remains open today. If we really touch poverty in whatever form it manifests itself, then it in turn will touch our hearts with the gift of faith.

Oh God, who rose again that all might believe and find eternal life, grant me the will to reach out when I do not want to, the love to comfort when I am rejected, the grace to see even in the darkness and the faith to believe in the midst of doubt.

JESUS MY PATIENT

Dearest Lord
May I see you today
and every day
in the person of your sick
and whilst nursing them,
minister unto you.

Though you hide yourself
behind the unattractive disguise
of the irritable,
the exacting,
the unreasonable,
may I still recognize you and say:
'Jesus, my patient, how sweet it is to serve you.'

Lord,
give me this seeing faith,
then my work will never be monotonous.
I will ever find new joy
in humouring the fancies
and gratifying the wishes
of all poor sufferers.

O Beloved Sick,
How doubly dear you are to me
when you personify Christ;
and what a privilege is mine
to be allowed to tend you.

Sweetest Lord,
Make me appreciative of the dignity of my high
vocation
And its many responsibilities.
Never permit me to disgrace it
by giving way to coldness,
unkindness,
or impatience.

And Oh God,
While you are Jesus,
my Patient,
deign also to be to me a patient Jesus,
bearing with my faults,
looking only to my intention
which is to love and serve you
in the person of each of your sick.

Lord,
Increase my faith,
bless my efforts and work,
now and for evermore.
AMEN

(Prayer offered daily by Mother Teresa's helpers in Shishu
Bhavan, Calcutta)

I am the vine, ye are the branches.

The fifteenth chapter of St John will bring us close
to Christ. This chapter of St John I think is so
fitting for us because the branch on the vine is
exactly what every Co-Worker is. The Father,
being the gardener, has to prune that branch to be
able to bring forth much fruit and the fruit that
we have to bring into the world is very beautiful
– the love of the Father (as the Father has loved
me, so I have loved you) and joy (abide in me that
my joy may be in you). Each one of us is a branch.

When I was last in Rome I wanted to give a little
instruction to my novice Sisters and I thought that
this chapter was the most beautiful means of
understanding what we are to Jesus and what
Jesus is to us. But I had not realized as those
young Sisters had realized when they looked at
the joining of the vine and the branches that the
joining was so tight – as if the vine were afraid
that something or somebody would separate the
branch from it.

The other thing that the Sisters drew my attention to was that when they looked at the vine they
could see no fruit. All the fruit was on the
branches. Then they told me that the humility of
Jesus is so great that he needs the branch to
produce the fruit. That is why he has taken so
much care over the joining – to be able to produce
that fruit he has made it a joining that somebody

59

will have to use force to separate. The Father, the gardener, prunes the branch to bring more fruit and the branch silently, lovingly, unconditionally, lets itself be pruned. We know what the pruning is for in all our lives there must be the cross and the closer we are to him the greater is the touch of the cross, and the pruning is much more intimate and delicate.

Each one of us is a Co-Worker of Christ, the branch on that vine, so what does it mean for you and me to be a Co-Worker of Christ? It means to abide in his love, to have his joy, to spread his compassion, to be a witness to his presence in the world.

May we be fruitful witnesses to the compassion, the love and the joy of Christ, to those nearest to us and to the world in which we live, through him whose care is infinite. Amen

Think not that I am come to send peace on earth: I came not to send peace, but a sword.

MATT. 10.34

The following of Christ is inseparable from the cross of Calvary. Do you think that I have come to bring peace on earth? No, I tell you but rather division! To those who follow Christ fully is given the world's hatred, for they are a challenge to his spirit just as Christ himself was hated first. Humiliation, lack of appreciation, criticism – we must remember that the people whom he healed or forgave turned round and crucified him.

Failure is nothing but the kiss of Jesus.

Have compassion even in the face of adversity. See the compassion of Christ towards Judas, the man who received so much love, yet betrayed his own master – the master who kept silent and would not betray him to his companions. Jesus could have easily spoken in public and told the others of the hidden intentions and deeds of Judas but he did not do so. He rather showed mercy and charity and, instead of condemning him, he called him a friend; and if Judas would have only looked into the eyes of Jesus as Peter did, today Judas would have been the friend of God's mercy. Jesus always had compassion.

In his passion Jesus taught us to forgive out of love, how to forget out of humility. So let us examine our hearts and see if there is any unforgiven hurt – any unforgotten bitterness!

If we suffer, we shall also reign with him.

2 TIM. 2.12

Today the world is an 'open Calvary'. Mental and physical suffering is everywhere. Pain and suffering have to come into your life but remember pain, sorrow, suffering are but the kiss of Jesus – signs that you have come so close to him that he can kiss you. Accept them as his gift – all for Jesus. You are really reliving the passion of Christ so accept Jesus as he comes into your life – bruised, divided, full of pains and wounds.

The spirit pours love, peace, joy into our hearts proportionately to our emptying ourselves of self-indulgence, vanity, anger and ambition, and to our willingness to shoulder the cross of Christ.

Without our suffering, our work would just be social work, very good and helpful, but it would not be the work of Jesus Christ, not part of the Redemption. Jesus wanted to help us by sharing our life, our loneliness, our agony and death. All that he has taken upon himself and has carried it into the darkest night. Only by being one with us has he redeemed us. We are allowed to do the same; all the desolation of the poor people, not only their material poverty, but their spiritual destitution must be redeemed; and we must share it, for only by being with them can we redeem them, that is by bringing God into their lives and bringing them to God.

Suffering in itself is nothing: but suffering

shared with Christ's passion is a wonderful gift. Man's most beautiful gift is that he can share in the passion of Christ. Yes, a gift and a sign of his love, because this is how his Father proved that he loved the world – by giving his son to die for us.

And so in Christ it was proved that the greatest gift is love because suffering was how he paid for sin.

Suffering, if it is accepted together, borne together, is joy. Remember that the passion of Christ ends always in the joy of the resurrection of Christ, so when you feel in your own heart the suffering of Christ, remember the resurrection has to come – the joy of Easter has to dawn. Never let anything so fill you with sorrow as to make you forget the joy of the risen Christ.

I have found you in so many places, Lord. I have felt your heartbeat in the perfect stillness of the open fields, in the shadowy tabernacle of an empty cathedral, in the oneness of heart and mind of an assembly of people who love you and fill the arches of your church with hymns and with love.

I have found you in joy. I search for you and often I find you. But in suffering I always find you. Suffering of any kind, is like the sound of the bell summoning God's bride to prayer.

When the shadow of the cross appears the soul recollects itself inwardly and, forgetful of the sound of the bell, it 'sees' you and speaks with you.

It is you who come to visit me and I answer you, 'Here I am, Lord. I have looked for you. I have longed for you . . .' In this meeting the soul no longer feels its suffering, but seems to be enraptured with your love, completely filled by you, suffused with you. I in you and you in me, that we may be one.

Then once again I open my eyes to life, a life less real now that I am divinely strengthened to follow your way.

Lord, I have found you in the terrible magnitude of the suffering of others. I have seen you in the sublime acceptance and unaccountable joy of those whose lives are racked with pain and I have heard your voice in the words of those whose personal agony mysteriously increases their selfless concern for other people.

But in my own niggling aches and petty sorrows I have failed to find you. I have lost the drama of your great redemptive passion in my own mundane weariness and the joyful life of Easter is submerged in the drabness of self-preoccupation.

Lord, I believe. Help thou my unbelief.

Wherever there are two, they are not without God, and where there is one alone, I say I am with him. Raise the stone and there thou shalt find me; cleave the wood and there I am. Let not him who seeks cease until he finds, and when he finds he shall be astonished. Astonished he shall reach the kingdom, and having reached the kingdom, he shall rest.

The Oxyrhynchus Sayings of Jesus

There is much suffering in the world – very much. And this material suffering is suffering from hunger, suffering from homelessness, from all kinds of diseases, but I still think the greatest suffering is being lonely, feeling unloved, just having no one. I have come more and more to realize that it is being unwanted that is the worst disease that any human being can ever experience. Nowadays we have found medicine for leprosy and lepers can be cured. There's medicine for TB and consumptives can be cured. For all kinds of diseases there are medicines, and cures, but for being unwanted, except where there are willing hands to serve and there's a loving heart to love, I don't think this terrible disease can ever be cured.

Let us recall what Christ said: 'Whatever you do to

the least of these, you do to me.' Jesus acts on both sides. On one side he is the person in need of help and on the other the one who gives help. Again he has said: 'Lo, I am with you alway, even to the end of the world.' This means that those who are alone need never feel totally abandoned and that those who offer love to the lonely become the means of fulfilling Christ's promise, at one with his love.

Through our meetings and our actions of love for our neighbour, in care for the sick and the lonely, the Lord Jesus is ever present among us. The Christ in man is there for the finding whether it be in ourselves or in others.

Lord, give me everyone who is sick or lonely . . .
I have felt in my heart the passion that fills
Your heart for the forsaken state of the world.

I love everyone who is sick or lonely . . .
I have felt in my heart the passion that fills
Your heart for the forsaken state of the world.

Let me be, in this world, my God, the tangible sacrament of your love. Let me be your arms that embrace and transform the loneliness of the world into love.

Often the key word in our encounter with loneliness is availability – availability by just listening, or by just giving a smile, or by just being truly present to those whom we meet in our daily lives.

Often too, we know the lonely, we recognize their isolation, we catch a glimpse of Christ in his most distressing disguise and we fail to reach out in love.

We may be trapped in our own isolation. We may be shy or reserved or lacking in confidence and so find it hard to show love easily. Indeed, we may feel that we are being insincere if we try to do so. Then let us accept ourselves as we are – God's imperfect instruments – and pray that he will use us, despite our shortcomings, in his plan of love for the world.

Come, Holy Spirit, give us hearts of peace and warmth which can serve as a refuge for those who suffer.
Come help us to be present one to another.

Jean Vanier

May the joy of the risen Jesus Christ be with you. To bring joy into our very soul the good God has given himself to us. In Bethlehem, 'joy' said the angel. In his life, he wanted to share his joy with his Apostles 'that my joy may be in you'. Joy was the password of the first Christians. St Paul – how often he repeated himself: 'Rejoice in the Lord alway: and again I say, rejoice.' In return for the great grace of baptism the priest tells the newly baptized: 'May you serve the Church joyfully.' Joy is not simply a matter of temperament in the service of God and souls. It is always hard – all the more reason why we should try to acquire it and make it grow in our hearts.

Joy is prayer – joy is strength – joy is love, joy is a net of love by which you can catch souls.

St Paul says: 'Each one must do as he has made up his mind, not reluctantly or under compulsion, for God loves a cheerful giver' (RSV). He gives most who gives with joy. If in your work you have difficulties and you accept them with joy, with a big smile – in this, as in any other thing, they will see your good works and glorify the Father. The best way to show your gratitude to God and people is to accept everything with joy. A joyful heart is the normal result of a heart burning with love.

Happiness is the axle of our religious life. A religious who is happy is like the sun in the community. Happiness is also the sign of a generous person. It is often the mantle that hides a life of sacrifice. Those who have the gift of happiness reach the peaks of perfection.

We must make sure that the sick and suffering find in us authentic angels of comfort and consolation. Why has our work in the slums been blessed by God? Not because of personal qualities but because of the happiness that certain nuns show. What we have – the faith, and being convinced that we are the sons of God – the people of the world do not have, especially those who live in the slums. Our joy is the surest means to announce Christianity to the world. What would our life be if nuns were not happy? Slavery and nothing else. We would go to work but attract no one.

Joy shows from the eyes, it appears when one speaks and walks. It cannot be kept closed inside us. It reacts outside. When people find in your eyes that habitual happiness, they will understand that they are the beloved children of God. Try to imagine a nun who goes to the slums with a sad face and uncertain step. What would her presence give to those people? Only more depression.

The coming of Jesus in Bethlehem brought joy to the world and every human heart. The same Jesus comes again and again in our hearts during Holy Communion. He wants to give the same joy and peace. May his coming bring to each one of us that peace and joy which he desires to give. Let us pray much for this grace in our own hearts, our communities and in the Church.

To know the Poor, we must know what is poverty;
To love the Poor, we must love until it hurts;
To serve the Poor, we must give whole-hearted free service.
Let us help each other by praying for each other – that we may have the joy of accepting the gift of God, to be his co-worker.

Lord,
We long for the Infinite and we feel the sorrow of things that pass away.
Remind us ever that beyond the tears of mankind there is the rainbow of joy,
That we may love the Infinite in all and so find joy in everything.

From a Hindu Co-Worker

And she brought forth her firstborn son, and wrapped him in swaddling clothes, and laid him in a manger; because there was no room for them in the inn.

LUKE 2.7

Each time Jesus wanted to prove his love for us, he was rejected by mankind. Before his birth, his parents asked for a simple dwelling place and there was none. At Christmas Christ comes like a little child, so small, so helpless, so much in need of all that love can give. Are we ready to receive him? If Mary and Joseph were looking for a place to make a home for Jesus, would they choose our house and all that it holds and is filled with?

Today there is so much trouble in the world and I think that much of it begins at home. The world is suffering so much because there is no peace. There is no peace because there is no peace in the family and we have so many thousands and thousands of broken homes. We must make our homes centres of compassion and forgive endlessly and so bring peace.

Make your house, your family another Nazareth where love, peace, joy and unity reign, for love begins at home. You must start there and make your home the centre of burning love. You must be the hope of eternal happiness to your wife, your husband, your child, to your grandfather, grandmother, to whoever is connected with you.

Do you know the poor of your own home first? Maybe in your home there is somebody who is

feeling very lonely, very unwanted, very handicapped. Maybe your husband, your wife, your
child is lonely. Do you know that? Where are the
old people today? They are put into institutions.
Why? Because they are unwanted, they are a
burden. I remember some time ago I visited a very
wonderful home for old people. There were about
forty there and they had everything, but they were
all looking towards the door. There was not a
smile on their faces and I asked the Sister in
charge of them: 'Sister, why are these people not
smiling? Why are they looking towards the door?'
And she, very beautifully, had to answer and give
the truth: 'It's the same every day. They are
longing for someone to come and visit them.' This
is great poverty.

I remember also, once I picked up a woman
from a dustbin and I knew she was dying. I took
her out and took her to the convent. She kept on
repeating the same words: 'My son did this to me'.
Not once did she utter the words: 'I'm hungry',
'I'm dying', 'I'm suffering'. She just kept on
repeating: 'My son did this to me'. It took me a
long time to help her to say: 'I forgive my son',
before she died.

The home is where the mother is. Once I picked
up a child and took him to our children's home,
gave him a bath, clean clothes, everything, but
after a day the child ran away. He was found again
by somebody else but again he ran away. Then I
said to the Sisters: 'Please follow that child. One
of you stay with him and see where he goes when

he runs away.' And the child ran away a third time. There under a tree was the mother. She had put two stones under a small earthenware vessel and was cooking something that she had picked up from the dustbins. The Sister asked the child: 'Why did you run away from the home?' And the child said: 'But this is my home because this is where my mother is'.

Mother was there. That was home. That the food was taken from the dustbins was all right because mother had cooked it. It was mother that hugged the child, mother who wanted the child and the child had its mother. Between a wife and a husband it is the same.

Smile at one another. It is not always easy. Sometimes I find it hard to smile at my Sisters but then we must pray. Prayer begins at home and a family that prays together, stays together. We must give Jesus a home in our homes for only then can we give him to others.

It is Christmas every time you smile at your brother and offer him your hand, every time you remain silent to listen to another, every time you turn your back on the principles that relegate the oppressed to the fringes of their isolation, every time you hope with the 'prisoners', those who are weighed down by the burden of physical, moral or spiritual poverty, every time you recognize in humility your limitations and your weakness.

It is Christmas every time you let God love others through you.

73

Let us pray that we shall be able to welcome Jesus at Christmas not in the cold manger of our heart but in a heart full of love and humility, a heart warm with love for one another.

*Now it came to pass, as they went, that he entered into
a certain village: and a certain woman named Martha
received him into her house.*

*And she had a sister called Mary, which also sat at
Jesus' feet, and heard his word.*

*But Martha was cumbered about much serving, and
came to him, and said, Lord, dost thou not care that my
sister hath left me to serve alone? bid her therefore that
she help me.*

*And Jesus answered and said unto her Martha,
Martha, thou art careful and troubled about many
things:*

*But one thing is needful: and Mary hath chosen
that good part, which shall not be taken away from
her.*

LUKE 10.38–42

*To everything there is a season, and a time to every
purpose under the heaven.*

ECCLES. 3.1

**Today we have no time even to look at each other,
to talk to each other, to enjoy each other, and still
less to be what our children expect from us, what
the husband expects from the wife, what the wife
expects from the husband. And so less and less
we are in touch with each other. The world is lost
for want of sweetness and kindness. People are
starving for love because everybody is in such a
great rush.**

Mother Teresa has said that we must find time, we must make time to be with the Lord in prayer. She has also directed us to pray the work. It follows that we must create time in our frequently all too busy lives for those works of selfless love which represent the mysterious fusion of prayer and action. It is a question only of priorities – of giving precedence not to a preoccupation with transitory considerations but to love and the glimpse it never fails to offer of the infinite. To everything there is a season; only love is a fruit in season at all times. And so when we are called upon to choose between personal preoccupations and wholehearted attention to others, let us give of that most precious of all commodities – our time. Strangely, if we do so, we will invariably find that tomorrow we can look upon the anxieties of today with renewed tranquillity.

The Lord is my pace setter . . . I shall not rush
He makes me stop for quiet intervals
He provides me with images of stillness which restore my serenity
He leads me in the way of efficiency through calmness of mind and his guidance is peace
Even though I have a great many things to accomplish each day, I will not fret, for his presence is here
His timelessness, his all importance will keep me in balance
He prepares refreshment and renewal in the midst of my activity by anointing my mind with his oils of tranquillity

My cup of joyous energy overflows
Truly harmony and effectiveness shall be the fruits of
my hours for I shall walk in the Pace of my Lord and
dwell in his house for ever.

A version of the 23rd Psalm from Japan

Beloved, if God so loved us, we ought also to love one another.
No man hath seen God at any time. If we love one another, God dwelleth in us, and his love is perfected in us.
Hereby know we that we dwell in him, and he in us, because he hath given us his Spirit.

1 JOHN 4:11–13

Christian unity is very important because Christians stand as a light for the world. If we are Christian we must be Christlike. Ghandi once said that if Christians lived their Christian life to the full there would be no Hindus left in India. That is what people expect of us, that we live our Christian life to the full.

The first Christians died for Jesus and they were recognized because they loved one another, and the world has never needed more love than today.

So often it is assumed that Church unity depends upon the reconciliation of Church leaders. Yet if we call ourselves Christians then we are all individually committed to being Christlike, and how can we fulfil this commitment if we fail to be in accord with that which is of Christ in all our fellow Christians? Unity like charity must surely begin with those small acts of openness, forgiveness and understanding undertaken with great love – if necessary in the home.

78

We are both of us challenged by the suffering of the modern world. Confronted with all that wounds humanity, we find the division between Christians unbearable. Are we ready to set aside our separations, freeing ourselves from our fear of one another? When people differ, what use is there in trying to find who was right and who was wrong?

In our search for reconciliation, are we ready to learn ways of offering the best of ourselves, of welcoming what is best in others, loving each other in the way Jesus loves us?

We thank you, Christ Jesus, because the Catholic Church is the Church of the Eucharist, rooted in your words, 'This is my body, this is my blood', so giving life to your adorable presence.

We thank you because the Protestant Churches are the Churches of the Word and constantly recall the power of your Gospel.

We thank you because the Orthodox Churches, so often in their history, are brought by faithfulness to go to the very extremes of loving.

So Christ, give us all openness to ways leading beyond our own selves: may we no longer delay reconciliation in that unique communion called the Church, irreplaceable leaven set in the midst of humanity.

Oh God, the father of all,
You ask every one of us to spread
Love where the poor are humiliated,
Joy where the Church is brought low,
And reconciliation where people are divided . . .

Father against son, mother against daughter, husband against wife,
Believers against those who cannot believe,
Christians against their unloved fellow Christians.

You open this way for us, so that the wounded body of Jesus Christ, your Church, may be leaven
for the poor of the earth and in the whole human family.

Mother Teresa and *Brother Roger* of Taizé

And I say unto you, That many shall come from the east and west, and shall sit down with Abraham, and Isaac, and Jacob, in the kingdom of heaven.

MATT. 8.11

Our purpose is to take God and his love to the poorest of the poor, irrespective of their ethical origin or the faith that they profess. Our discernment of aid is not the belief but the necessity. We never try to convert those who receive to Christianity but in our work we bear witness to the love of God's presence and if Catholics, Protestants, Buddhists or agnostics become for this better men – simply better – we will be satisfied. Growing up in love they will be nearer to God and will find him in his goodness.

Every human being comes from the hand of God and we all know what is the love of God for us. My religion is everything to me but for every individual, according to the grace God has given that soul. God has his own ways and means to work in the hearts of men and we do not know how close they are to him but by their actions we will always know whether they are at his disposal or not. Whether you are a Hindu, a Moslem or a Christian, how you live your life is the proof that you are fully his or not. We must not condemn or judge or pass words that will hurt people. Maybe a person has never heard of Christianity. We do not know what way God is appearing to that soul and what way God is drawing that soul, and therefore who are we to condemn anybody?

It matters to the individual what Church he belongs to. If that individual thinks and believes that this is the only way to God for her or him, this is the way God comes into their life – his life. If he does not know any other way and if he has no doubt so that he does not need to search then this is his way to salvation. This is the way God comes into his life. But the moment a soul has the grace to know and to want to know more about God, more about faith, more about religion, then he has to search and if he does not search then he goes astray. God gives to every soul that he has created a chance to come face to face with him, to accept him or reject him.

People throughout the world may look different, or have a different religion, education or position, but they are all the same. They are all people to be loved. They are all hungry for love. The people you see in the streets of India or Hong Kong are hungry in body, but the people in London or New York have also a hunger which must be satisfied. Every person needs to be loved.

Some call him Ishwar, some call him Allah, some simply God, but we all have to acknowledge that it is he who made us for greater things: to love and to be loved. What matters is that we love. We cannot love without prayer and so whatever religion we are we must pray together.

Whatever his creed, there is only one possible way for man to attain to the life of God in the soul. God is one, human nature is one, salvation is one and the way to it lies in the desire of the soul turned towards God.

May I never cause pain to any living being.
May I never utter untruth, and
May I never covet the wealth or wife of another.
May I ever drink the nectar of contentment.
May I always entertain a feeling of friendliness for all living beings in the world.
May the spring of sympathy in my heart be ever bubbling to those in agony and affliction.
May I never feel angry with the vile, the vicious and the wrongly directed.
May there be an adjustment of things that I shall always remain tranquil in dealing with them.

Whether people speak of me well or ill
Whether wealth comes to me or departs
Whether I live to be hundreds of thousands of years old
or give up the spirit this day
Whether anyone holds out any kind of fears
Or with worldly riches he tempts me
In the face of all these possible things
May my footsteps swerve not from the path of truth.

With pleasure may the mind not be puffed up
Let pain disturb it never
May the awesome loneliness of a mountain, forest or river
Or a burning place, never cause it to shiver,

Unmoved, unshakeable, in firmness may it grow
adamantine
And display true moral strength when parted from the
desired thing,
Or united with the undesired.
May there be mutual love in the world.
May delusion dwell at a distance
May no one ever utter unpleasant speech
Or words that are harsh lies ensue
May all understand the Laws of Truth
and joyfully sorrow and sufferings endure
Om, peace, Shanti, Shanti, Shanti.

Extract from the Contemplation in the Shire Digambar
Jain Temple in celebration of the Silver Jubilee of the
Missionaries of Charity.

Peace I leave with you, my peace I give unto you:
not as the world giveth, give I unto you.

JOHN 14.27

Let us thank God for his gift of peace that reminds us that we have been created to live that peace, and that Jesus became man in all things like us except in sin, and he proclaimed very clearly that he had come to give the good news. The news was peace to all men of good will and this is something that we all want – peace of heart.

Let us preach the peace of Christ as he did. He went about doing good. He did not stop his works of charity because the Pharisees and others hated him or tried to spoil his Father's work. He just went about doing good. Cardinal Newman wrote: 'Help me to spread thy fragrance everywhere I go – let me preach thee without preaching, not by words but by my example.' Our works of love are nothing but the works of peace.

Let us not use bombs and guns to overcome the world. Let us use love and compassion. Peace begins with a smile – smile five times a day at someone you don't really want to smile at at all – do it for peace. So let us radiate the peace of God and so light his light and extinguish in the world and in the hearts of all men all hatred and love for power.

Everywhere we come up against boundaries – now between races and social layers, now between religions.

There are curtains of iron, there are walls of ice, there are deep ravines between people who cannot understand one another. Those on the other side do not concern us. If we can avoid having anything to do with them, then that is the best, we think.

It was to this world that Jesus came and with him came something quite different. He was not concerned about the many ridiculous boundaries that people had drawn up among themselves or rather, he came in order to go beyond and do away with these boundaries. The love and care of the God he revealed did not make any distinction between people. Regardless of where they lived – in Judaea or Samaria, whether they worshipped on Gerizim or in Jerusalem – they were all in the same plight, and had all the same value. Jesus had come to seek and save that which was lost, he was the shepherd looking after the lost and the lost were everywhere.

The love that we meet in Jesus is the love that overcomes all boundaries and it is the same love that we find reflected in those who, throughout the history of the Church, have tried to follow in their Master's footsteps.

If there is something that our divided world without peace needs then it is people who in the name of Christ will cross boundaries to lessen their neighbour's need, regardless of standing and reputation. Blessed are the merciful, said Jesus.

It is this care without boundaries, this understanding of the worth of man, this desire to heal the broken – it is this that after all lies at the bottom of all peacemaking work, regardless of where it is done and by whom.

From the sermon given in Oslo Cathedral by the vice-chairman of the Nobel Committee following the presentation to Mother Teresa of the Nobel Prize for Peace

Lead me from death to life,
   from falsehood to truth;
Lead me from despair to hope,
   from fear to trust;
Lead me from hate to love,
   from war to peace;
Let peace fill our heart, our world,
   our universe

Prayer for peace by *Satish Kumar*

Lord, make me a channel of thy peace that, where there is hatred, I may bring love; that where there is wrong, I may bring the spirit of forgiveness; that, where there is discord, I may bring harmony; that, where there is error, I may bring truth; that, where there is despair, I may bring hope; that, where there are shadows I may bring light; that, where there is sadness, I may bring joy.

Prayer of St Francis

Keep the light of Christ always burning in your heart – for he alone is the Way to walk. He is the Life to live. He is the Love to love.

Free Public Library
Livingston, N. J.

Offers of help and inquiries relating to the work of Mother Teresa, the Missionaries of Charity and the Co-Workers should be addressed to:

The Missionaries of Charity

149 George Street
Fitzroy 3065
Melbourne
Victoria
AUSTRALIA

177 Bravington Road
London W9
ENGLAND

335 East 145th Street
Bronx
New York 10451
U.S.A.

54a Lower Circular Road
Calcutta – 700016
WEST BENGAL

The Co-Worker Links for any of the countries mentioned and for any neighbouring countries can also be contacted c/o the addresses above.

840203